Felix Ale

Review about Gregg Bradens "Fractal Time". A Clue to Human History

GRIN Publishing

Imprint:

Copyright © 2014 GRIN Verlag GmbH
Print and binding: Books on Demand GmbH, Norderstedt Germany
ISBN: 978-3-656-89305-9

This book at GRIN:

http://www.grin.com/en/e-book/289013/review-about-gregg-bradens-fractal-time-a-clue-to-human-history

GRIN - Your knowledge has value

Since its foundation in 1998, GRIN has specialized in publishing academic texts by students, college teachers and other academics as e-book and printed book. The website www.grin.com is an ideal platform for presenting term papers, final papers, scientific essays, dissertations and specialist books.

Visit us on the internet:

http://www.grin.com/

http://www.facebook.com/grincom

http://www.twitter.com/grin_com

ALE FELIX BABATUNDE

"FRACTAL TIME ESSAY"- A CLUE TO HUMAN HISTORY.

ATLANTIC INTERNATIONAL UNIVERSITY

SUBMITTED:
14TH DECEMBER, 2014.

The book "Fractal Time-The Secret of 2012 and the New World Age" by Gregg Braden explores the discoveries of time as the means of communication from the past. In addition, the book proposes that time defines the map to an individual's future and provides a picture of the world to come. The Mayans identify December 21, 2012 as the end of the world age, particularly to be attributed to the Winter solace. The cycle is predicted to have started in the 5th world age that is approximately 3114 B.C. This defines 1800 years prior the time of the exodus of Moses, which is around 5125 years ago. Parallel to the world-age the traditions of the Indians were passing on through oral traditions thus they may have lost their accuracy along the transmission. Therefore, the oral communications are dated back before the literature.

The four generations that have passed through the end of the world age have been found to have survived the alterations in the climate and the global magnetic field. Therefore, I believe that the rise in the sea levels and the lowered availability of resources for one age presents an opportunity for the next world age. Therefore, it is important to complete the cycle prior to commencing the following cycle. This translates to mean that the earth will experience the greatest distance of its orbit from the harboring galaxy the milky way.

The prophesies made in 2012 proposed that the earth would end, and humankind would be swept away by tidal forces, parallel to historical predictions. However, the author suggests that we are approaching a period where humans will be able to make decisions that can alter our future. I believe that we can use the eye-opening finding of John Braden to modify the results of our future.

It is important to acknowledge that the Mayans failed to examine the beginnings and end of history. There are various propositions on the end of the world from different cultures and religion all over the world. This means that the end of the world is bound to come. In addition, there are various geographical trends such as global warming that have shown that the world fails to be self-sustaining and that continuous destruction of the earth will lead to the demise.Gregg shows that the melting ice caps are merely a part of the cycle through taking global warming as a function of air pollution.The decision of the industry in Japan to release greenhouse gasses into the atmosphere is bound to affect an individual in Egypt. Therefore, it is evident that the actions of every person on the earth is interconnected.

There is an apparent relation between the spiritual and emotional effects, and the physical changes, that bring about a sense of loss of interconnection leading to separation and being lost. It has been noted that the increased distance between the source of the powerful energy. This means leading the ancestors to chaos, greed, warm destruction, and war. The primary theme of the time of great darkness during the period of great darkness that may be noted at the end of the world is contention, discord, and quarrel. Regardless of the fear of the negative results, our ancestors are observed to have had an awareness of the existence of intense love, peace, compassion, and healing.

Currently, the technology and the understanding of our needs provides us with choices; thus, the different possibilities are expected to mold our future. The solar system and the earth move into alignment, thus creating an imaginary line, which defines the bottom of the equator and the top of the galaxy as the Southern and Northern hemisphere, where the source of energy is attributed to the center of the Milky way. The winter solstice of 2012 was predicted to be the central transition region, which started prior and after 12/21, where each of the sides was constituted of a number of years. The Mayans predicted the alignment to be sequential with a range of 26,000 years that represented the movement through 12 zodiac constellations and signs, thus creating a circular path of 360 degrees.

There is a need to update our understanding of time and; consequently, increase our time concepts. The ancient cultures observed time as a continuous wave of cycles caused by waves of energy that were derived from the universe. This produced patterns through a range of dimensions and fractals that harbored conditions of the past; however, the fractals were noted to have greater intensity in determining the future.

The famous scientist Albert Einstein proposed the unity of time and space that was referred to as space-time. This determined the occurrences of everyday life on the various aspects of life including the economy, war and peace, civilizations, social relations and the cosmos that are observed within the space-time. The fractal interrelation between galaxies, planets and the lives of humans is directly associated with the ancient relation that proposes parallelism between above and below.

The cycles that are observed in nature have different levels of effects, including the small patterns present in protons and neutrons to the galaxies, in the progressive nature of cycles. It is evident that the life of different humans fails to reveal the truth; therefore, nature has proven to be limitless leading to the conclusion that every end is a beginning. The occurrences within each cycle may be considered as a seed event. Thus, it is the subsequent occurrence of a condition that renders a given outcome possible, which is reliant on the various choices that we make in our lives. Therefore, it is possible to predict future occurrences through acknowledging our position in the cycle.

The proposition is relative not only to the various cosmological changes but also to personal occurrences and global wars. In the book, Braden has provided a Time Code Calculator, which illustrates possible human expectations. Using the current technology, it is possible to predict the choice point, and cyclical alterations thus permitting us to formulate a new result to restore the pattern conditions. It is important to understand the Phi/phi, defined as 1.618:0.618. This is referred to as the golden ratio that is repetitive in infinity and the architectural fields.

Fibonacci noted that in the early 14th century, the sequence of digits, which formed the golden ratio, with addition of the final two digits led to expansion into a spiral or the division of the number that occurs prior. Thus, the universe is noted to have a spiral pattern.

It may be concluded that the beauty that is present in the earth may be attributed to ratios. The examples of beauty related to ratios includes the human body, the structures of the Grecian temples, the patterns created by the seeds in a sunflower and the arms formed by the Milky Way galaxy. Ratios are also applicable to the proportions of DNA. Thus, the cycles of growth are present in the golden ration and the separation and timing of the events that are observed in the different occurrences in the personal life of a person.

It is evident that the only relationship that exists between humankind and time is the actions that take place within time. Therefore, time and human actions have proven to be conjoined and interrelated. Quantum physics evolved to categorize various zone of energy defined as probabilities.

Both the cycles of proportionality and growth are found to be present in the golden ratio. In addition, the golden ratio is present in the occurrence of events in the life of an individual. The only mechanism of relating to time is through the events that take place in our lives; therefore, events and time are inseparable. The Hopi, as the primary communication language, is applied in the explanation of the events that are happening at a particular time and the events that have taken place in the past.

Therefore, parallel to Albert Einstein's views, the present, future and past may be considered an illusion. Space and time have proven to create a wave, which moves sequentially thus forming a spiral shape. Consequently, a torsion field is created that can be used to predict the behavior of nature.

The convergence of numerous cycles provides an ideal time to start new patterns to facilitate growth. In our various personal lives, it presents a chance to let go of emotional scarring events and ensure that we place our lives on the track that we may wish. Therefore, humankind is required to cooperate with the world rather than demonstrate any form of competition. This shows that a change in our self-perception may potentially modify the world to suit our preferences. Using our hearts and feelings, we can adjust our bodies using the self-sustaining earth fields, which interconnect the humankind. Therefore, the theory proposes that attaining global parallelism in our political, social and economic views is bound to strengthen the bonds between us. This provides humanity with a choice to choose their future and modify the reaction of what we refer to as nature or fate.

If the propositions made in the novel are true, we can learn from the past and aim to make wiser choices to better our future. Our future is determined by the choices we make in our daily encounters, particularly our reactions to difference incidents of crisis in our lives. The propositions in the novel provide every individual with the chance of improving our lives in the world. The book provides the reader with a better understanding of the space/time continuum through the provision of information on the movement of spiral cycles that form the energy potential to fuel particular events. I believe that we can use the eye-opening finding of John Braden to modify the results of our future. Gregg demonstrates that cycles do not pose as destiny, but pose as opportunities. It is vital to acknowledge that the world we know will soon evolve and adopt a new form. We can all participate in the improvement of our political, economic and social lives. This will create a brighter future for all humankind in the earth.

References

Braden, G. (2009). *Fractal Time*. Hay House.